THE TEN COMMANDMENTS

FOUNDATIONS IN FAITH

Study Guide

SAINT LOUIS

Edited by Kenneth Wagener

This publication is available in braille and in large print for the visually impaired. Write to Library for the Blind, 1333 S. Kirkwood Rd., St. Louis, MO 63122-7295; or call 1-800-433-3954.

Scripture quotations taken from the HOLY BIBLE, NEW INTERNATIONAL VERSION®. NIV®. Copyright © 1973, 1978, 1984 by International Bible Society. Used by permission of Zondervan Publishing House. All rights reserved.

Quotations of the Small Catechism are from *Luther's Small Catechism with Explanation*, copyright © 1986, 1991 by Concordia Publishing House.

Quotations from the Large Catechism are from *Luther's Large Catechism. A Contemporary Translation*, copyright © 1978 by Concordia Publishing House.

"Pray Together" sections are taken from Leslie Brandt, *Psalms Now*, copyright © 1996 by Concordia Publishing House.

1 2 3 4 5 6 7 8 9 10   07 06 05 04 03 02 01 00 99 98

CONTENTS

INTRODUCTION

The Foundations in Faith series is an introduction to the truths of God's Word as presented in Luther's Small Catechism.

Why Study the Catechism?

In the early Christian church, God's people confessed their faith and witnessed to the world in brief creeds. "Jesus is Lord" (1 Corinthians 12:3). "The mystery of godliness is great: He appeared in a body, was vindicated by the Spirit, was seen by angels" (1 Timothy 3:16). These passages from the New Testament, along with others, gave believers short, concise statements of faith in Jesus as Savior and Lord. In time, the church wrote and adopted new creeds to explain more fully the basics of the Christian faith.

The church also wrote and adopted catechisms as summaries of the major doctrines of Holy Scripture. At first, catechisms were tools for teachers. With the invention of the printing press, catechisms were printed for pastors, teachers of the faith, and parents to use within the congregation and at home.

Luther's Small Catechism, published in 1529, covers the "six chief parts" of Christian doctrine. In Luther's words, "The Catechism is an epitome and brief transcript of the entire Holy Scripture." It is a summary and guide for believers, as they learn and reflect on the truths of God's Word.

The Foundations in Faith series explores Luther's Small Catechism in four parts: The Ten Commandments, The Apostles' Creed, The Lord's Prayer, and The Sacraments. The study guides may be used in any order (although the sequence in the catechism is preferred), and are designed as an *introduction* or *refresher* course for congregational or personal use. Ideally, participants will learn how the catechism presents God's Word in a clear, understandable way, in order to bring God's people to faith in Christ and to a daily life shaped and empowered by Word and Sacrament.

May God bless your study of His Word in the catechism!

THE FIRST 1 COMMANDMENT AND CONCLUSION TO THE COMMANDMENTS

Pray Together

My heart is full today.
I am so grateful for all that God has done for me.
I cannot see Him, but I can see the works of His
    hands.
He is a merciful and loving God.
He is a righteous and faithful God.
He is a majestic and powerful God.
He is a forgiving God.
He takes me back to His loving heart when I go
    astray.
He is in this world today.
And those who recognize and belong to Him
are building on foundations that are eternally
    secure.
How grateful I am to my God today! Amen.

Discover

God alone is God. In the Ten Commandments, God forbids all kinds of idolatry—worship of other gods. In Christ, our heavenly Father forgives our sin, and helps us to fear, love, and trust in Him throughout our lives.

Introduction

It's a fundamental concept in business, sports, and management: *Keep the main thing the main thing.*

What's first in my life? What is my ultimate priority?

It's a critical question in all facets of life.

- From your experience, what is *the main thing* for many people in our world today?

- In what ways does the main thing in our life often shape everything else in life?

The Ten Commandments are God's Law. At creation, God "wrote" His Law on human hearts. Adam and Eve knew, accepted, and lived God's Law perfectly. They trusted God and reflected His will in their thoughts, words, and actions.

Yet Adam and Eve sinned; they disobeyed God's Word and plunged the world into rebellion and brokenness. (See Romans 5:12–21, where we are reminded that one sin resulted in the condemnation of all people.) Since the fall in Eden, all human beings are *unable* to keep God's Law perfectly and *unwilling* to listen to and obey His Word. The Ten Commandments, as a summary of God's holy, righteous will, tell us what to do and what not to do.

God gave the Ten Commandments to Moses at Mount Sinai. He revealed His will for His covenant people in the two tablets of the Law: "When the LORD finished speaking to Moses on Mount Sinai, He gave him the two tablets of the Testimony, the tablets of stone inscribed by the finger of God" (Exodus 31:18).

It's helpful today to divide the Ten Commandments into two *tables:*

The First Table: Commandments 1–3
The Second Table: Commandments 4–10

The Catechism

THE FIRST COMMANDMENT
You shall have no other gods.

What does this mean? We should fear, love, and trust in God above all things.

People fear many things. People love and trust in many different things. The First Commandment confronts us with the main thing: fear, love, and trust in God *above all things.* The only true God is the triune God: Father, Son, and Holy Spirit.

Martin Luther notes in the Large Catechism: "The point of this commandment, therefore, is to require that kind of true faith and confidence of the heart that is directed toward the one true God and clings to Him alone. The meaning is: 'See to it that you let Me alone be your God, and never look about for another.' "

1. What images come to mind in the words *fear* God? *love* God? *trust* God?

2. Idolatry, at root, is placing other things above God. What kind of idols do we make and worship today?

3. Describe what it means to *cling* to God.

God's Word

When the people saw that Moses was so long in coming down from the mountain, they gathered around Aaron and said, "Come, make us gods who will go before us. As for this fellow Moses who brought us up out of Egypt, we don't know what has happened to him."

Aaron answered them, "Take off the gold earrings that your wives, your sons and your daughters are wearing, and bring them to me."

So all the people took off their earrings and brought them to Aaron. He took what they handed him and made it into an idol cast in the shape of a calf, fashioning it with a tool. Then they said, "These are your gods, O Israel, who brought you up out of Egypt."

When Aaron saw this, he built an altar in front of the calf and announced, "Tomorrow there will be a festival to the LORD."

So the next day the people rose early and sacrificed burnt offerings and presented fellowship offerings. Afterward they sat down to eat and drink and got up to indulge in revelry.

Then the LORD said to Moses, "Go down, because your people, whom you brought up out of Egypt, have become corrupt. They have been quick to turn away from what I commanded them and have made themselves an idol cast in the shape of a calf. They have bowed down to it and sacrificed to it and have said, 'These are your gods, O Israel, who brought you up out of Egypt.'

"I have seen these people," the LORD said to Moses, "and they are a stiff-necked people. Now leave Me alone so that My anger may burn against them and that I may destroy them. Then I will make you into a great nation."

But Moses sought the favor of the LORD his God. "O LORD," he said, "why should Your anger burn against Your people, whom You brought out of Egypt with great power and a mighty hand?" … Then the LORD relented and did not bring on His people the disaster He had threatened (Exodus 32:1–11, 14).

4. In what ways are people today like the people of Israel?

5. Why, from your experience, do people turn to idols?

6. What does the story reveal about God's attitude toward idolatry? toward His people?

God forbids us to have other gods. Whenever we regard people, possessions, status, or achievement as our highest priority in life, we worship idols. Whenever we worship any god other than the true God, we worship idols. Whenever we fear, love, and trust in any part of creation as the main thing, we worship idols.

In *The Ten Commandments* (St. Louis: Concordia, 1996), Norbert Oesch writes,

> The Israelites had a deliverer in Moses, who was sent by God to show them the way out of their bondage. So we too need a deliverer. Our sinfulness is like a slavery and bondage. We need to be delivered from it in order that God's vengeance and anger and wrath will not come upon us, that we will not be abandoned forever.
>
> God sent His Son Jesus Christ to be our deliverer. Jesus took upon Himself God's own wrath for our breaking the covenant … He suffered that vengeance, wrath, and abandonment in our place. As a result, our Lord God says, "Because restitution has been made, I make a new covenant with you, a covenant based upon the forgiveness of sins. I restore you to be My people. Now you are My sons and daughters; and despite your sin, I am

your God. I am your benefactor, and I will provide for you; I will care for you."

God also says, "Furthermore, I am giving you the power to love Me above everything else."

In Jesus, God forgives our idolatry and gives us His grace and strength to fear, love, and trust in Him in our lives.

- In what ways does faith in Christ enable you to *keep the main thing the main thing?*

- In what ways does faith in Christ shape everything in your life?

God's Word

Some time later God tested Abraham. He said to him, "Abraham!" "Here I am," he replied.

Then God said, "Take your son, your only son, Isaac, whom you love, and go to the region of Moriah. Sacrifice him there as a burnt offering on one of the mountains I will tell you about."

Early the next morning Abraham got up and saddled his donkey. He took with him two of his servants and his son Isaac. When he had cut enough wood for the burnt offering, he set out for the place God had told him about ...

Abraham took the wood for the burnt offering and placed it on his son Isaac, and he himself carried the fire and the knife. As the two of them went on together, Isaac spoke up and said to his father Abraham, "Father?"

"Yes, my son?" Abraham replied.

"The fire and wood are here," Isaac said, "but where is the lamb for the burnt offering?"

Abraham answered, "God Himself will provide the lamb for the burnt offering, my son." And the two of them went on together.

When they reached the place God had told him about, Abraham built an altar there and arranged the wood on it. He bound his son Isaac and laid him on the altar, on top of the wood. Then he reached out his hand and took the knife to slay his son. But the angel of the LORD called out to him from heaven, "Abraham! Abraham!"

"Here I am," he replied.

"Do not lay a hand on the boy," He said. "Do not do anything to him. Now I know that you fear God, because you have not withheld from Me your son, your only son."

Abraham looked up and there in a thicket he saw a ram caught by its horns. He went over and took the ram and sacrificed it as a burnt offering instead of his son. So Abraham called that place The LORD Will Provide. And to this day it is said, "On the mountain of the LORD it will be provided" (Genesis 22:1–3, 6–14).

7. Describe your thoughts and feelings about God's test for Abraham.

8. In what ways does Abraham demonstrate his complete trust in God?

9. How does the story of Abraham and Isaac remind you of the heavenly Father's sacrifice of His Son?

By God's grace, we live in faith, forgiven and renewed in Christ our Savior.

- We fear God above all things as we revere Him, honor Him with our thoughts, words, and actions, and seek to follow our Savior's will.
- We love God above all things as we cling to Him and devote ourselves to His care and service.
- We trust in God above all things as we commit ourselves completely to His goodness in Christ and rely on Him for all our needs.

The Catechism

The Close of the Commandments

What does God say about all these commandments? He says: "I, the Lord your God, am a jealous God, punishing the children for the sin of the fathers to the third and fourth generation of those who hate Me, but showing love to a thousand generations of those who love Me and keep My commandments." (Exodus 20:5–6)

What does this mean? God threatens to punish all who break these commandments. Therefore, we should fear His wrath and not do anything against them. But He promises grace and every blessing to all who keep these commandments. Therefore, we should also love and trust in Him and gladly do what He commands.

In his catechism, Luther used God's Word in Exodus 20:5–6 as an appendix to the Ten Commandments. The words, originally spoken by God to Moses, contain both "a threat of wrath to terrify and warn us and a friendly promise to attract us and to beckon us to take in and prize God's words of command" (Large Catechism).

As a jealous God, the heavenly Father hates sin and requires us to obey His commandments. He will not share His glory with idols. And He will punish all who reject and hate Him.

But in Christ God is compassionate and forgiving. He takes away our sin and guilt and gives us His strength to love and keep His commandments. In His mercy, He blesses us with His good gifts—above all, forgiveness, life, and salvation.

10. In our day some prefer the title *The Ten Suggestions.* In what ways do people no longer regard the Ten Commandments as serious or important?

11. Jesus alone has fulfilled God's Law—for us! How does His daily forgiveness help you through failures and hardships in your life?

12. What comfort do you have in knowing that God now invites us to "take in and prize" His commandments as His forgiven children in Christ?

God's People Pray

Heavenly Father,
in Your Son You delivered us from sin and death
and have forgiven us by Your grace.
Strengthen us by Your Holy Spirit.
Give us faith and hope every day.
Help us to hold fast to Your promises,
and guide us to love Your Word.
May we always fear, love, and trust in You
throughout our life.
To Your glory, through Christ we pray. Amen.

A Verse a Day

Sunday: Hear, O Israel: The LORD our God, the LORD is one. (Deuteronomy 6:4)

Monday: May the grace of the Lord Jesus Christ, and the love of God, and the fellowship of the Holy Spirit be with you all. (2 Corinthians 13:14)

Tuesday: I am the LORD; that is My name! I will not give My glory to another or My praise to idols. (Isaiah 42:8)

Wednesday: The fool says in his heart, "There is no God." They are corrupt, their deeds are vile; there is no one who does good. (Psalm 14:1)

Thursday: For great is the LORD and most worthy of praise; He is to be feared above all gods. (Psalm 96:4)

Friday: Jesus replied: "Love the Lord your God with all your heart and with all your soul and with all your mind." (Matthew 22:37)

Saturday: Trust in the LORD with all your heart and lean not on your own understanding; in all your ways acknowledge Him, and He will make your paths straight. (Proverbs 3:5–6)

14

THE SECOND AND THIRD COMMANDMENTS 2

Pray Together

You are my God.
You never let me out of Your sight.
Even when I strike out on my own,
You pursue me and hold on to me.
Thank You for taking me back, Lord,
for renewing my relationship with You.
I seek now to walk in Your course for me.
I shall proclaim Your praises and live out Your
    purposes.
Enable me to be faithful to You, whatever the
    consequences,
and to celebrate Your love
and communicate it to everyone around me. Amen.

Discover

God's name and Word are holy. In the Ten Commandments, God forbids us to misuse His name or despise His Word. In Christ, our heavenly Father forgives our sins and helps us to pray and worship as His chosen people.

Introduction

An ancient proverb suggests, "Speaking is a mirror of the soul; as we speak, so we are."

- Describe how what we say reveals who we are.

- In what ways does what we see and read shape who we are?

The Catechism

THE SECOND COMMANDMENT

You shall not misuse the name of the Lord your God.

What does this mean? We should fear and love God so that we do not curse, swear, use satanic arts, lie, or deceive by His name, but call upon it in every trouble, pray, praise, and give thanks.

God's name is good. God's name is holy. God's name reveals His identity, His nature, and His attributes.

Rudolph Norden writes in *Day by Day with Jesus* (St. Louis: Concordia, 1997): "Names are important. God has revealed Himself to us by name, not by number. His name is Yahweh, the Lord, the Almighty, God Most High, or, with reference to the Trinity, Father, Son, and Holy Spirit. God's name is not just a word tacked on, but it is God Himself as He has revealed Himself. ... God's name describes God as He is."

The Second Commandment shows that God's name is important: God wants us to use—to speak—His name as He has commanded in His Word.

16

1. In what ways do people misuse God's name today?

2. When have you called on God's name in trouble? in praise and thanksgiving?

3. Jesus means *Savior.* How does knowing Jesus as Savior encourage you to call on God's name in your need?

God's Word

Now Moses was tending the flock of Jethro his father-in-law, the priest of Midian, and he led the flock to the far side of the desert and came to Horeb, the mountain of God. There the angel of the LORD appeared to him in flames of fire from within a bush. Moses saw that though the bush was on fire it did not burn up.

So Moses thought, "I will go over and see this strange sight—why the bush does not burn up."

When the LORD saw that he had gone over to look, God called to him from within the bush, "Moses! Moses!"

And Moses said, "Here I am."

"Do not come any closer," God said. "Take off your sandals, for the place where you are standing is holy ground." Then He said, "I am the God of your father, the God of Abraham, the God of Isaac and the God of Jacob." At this, Moses hid his face, because he was afraid to look at God.

The LORD said, "I have indeed seen the misery of My people in Egypt. I have heard them crying out because of their slave drivers, and I am concerned about their suffering …"

"So now, go. I am sending you to Pharaoh to bring My people the Israelites out of Egypt." But Moses said to God, "Who am I, that I should go to Pharaoh and bring the Israelites out of Egypt?"

And God said, "I will be with you. And this will be the sign to you that it is I who have sent you: When you have brought the people out of Egypt, you will worship God on this mountain."

Moses said to God, "Suppose I go to the Israelites and say to them, 'The God of your fathers has sent me to you,' and they ask me, 'What is His name?' Then what shall I tell them?"

God said to Moses, "I AM WHO I AM. This is what you are to say to the Israelites: 'I AM has sent me to you' " (Exodus 3:1–7, 10–14).

4. What does God reveal about Himself in the burning bush? in the name "I AM WHO I AM"?

5. How does Moses recognize that he is unworthy to stand before God? that he is completely dependent on God's mercy?

6. How does God's promise encourage you in the tasks you have?

God's name is holy. We misuse His name when we speak it uselessly or carelessly, and when we

curse—speak evil of God or mock Him;

swear—speak an oath falsely, thoughtlessly, or in trivial matters;

use satanic arts—speak God's name in occult practices (fortune-telling, astrology, magic, etc.);

lie or deceive by His name—speak God's name in false teaching or hypocritically.

Though we have sinned against God in our speaking, thinking, and doing, He offers His rich forgiveness in Christ.

God's Word

Now on His way to Jerusalem, Jesus traveled along the border between Samaria and Galilee. As He was going into a village, ten men who had leprosy met Him. They stood at a distance and called out in a loud voice, "Jesus, Master, have pity on us!"

When He saw them, He said, "Go, show yourselves to the priests." And as they went, they were cleansed.

One of them, when he saw he was healed, came back, praising God in a loud voice. He threw himself at Jesus' feet and thanked Him—and he was a Samaritan.

Jesus asked, "Were not all ten cleansed? Where are the other nine? Was no one found to return and give praise to God except this foreigner?" Then He said to him, "Rise and go; your faith has made you well" (Luke 17:11–19).

7. "Jesus, Master, have pity on us!" What hardships would the ten lepers have faced in life?

8. Describe the differences between the nine lepers and the one leper.

9. In what ways does Jesus speak to us today, "Rise and go; your faith has made you well"?

Through Christ, we call on God's name in faith, asking His help in our troubles, praising Him for His goodness, and giving thanks for all His blessings.

The Catechism

THE THIRD COMMANDMENT
Remember the Sabbath day by keeping it holy.

What does this mean? We should fear and love God so that we do not despise preaching and His Word, but hold it sacred and gladly hear and learn it.

Sabbath means rest. After He created the heavens and the earth, God rested on the seventh day from all His work. The Scriptures report, "God blessed the seventh day and made it holy, because on it He rested from all the work of creating He had done" (Genesis 2:2–3).

In the Old Testament, the Sabbath was *Saturday.* It was a day of rest and a day devoted to hearing and meditating on God's Word. For the Christian church, *Sunday* is generally the day of rest and worship. Since Christ rose from the dead on Sunday, His people gather especially on Sunday to hear His Word and rest in His salvation.

10. How have attitudes toward Sunday as *the Lord's Day* changed in your lifetime?

11. How do God's people sin against the Third Commandment?

12. In what ways is the Sabbath rest for the *body?* for the *soul?*

God's Word

Every year Jesus' parents went to Jerusalem for the Feast of the Passover. When He was twelve years old, they went up to the Feast, according to the custom. After the Feast was over, while His parents were returning home, the boy Jesus stayed behind in Jerusalem, but they were unaware of it. Thinking He was in their company, they traveled on for a day. Then they began looking for Him among their relatives and friends. When they did not find Him, they went back to Jerusalem to look for Him. After three days they found Him in the temple courts, sitting among the teachers, listening to them and asking them questions. Everyone who heard Him was amazed at His understanding and His answers.

When His parents saw Him, they were astonished. His mother said to Him, "Son, why have You treated us like this? Your father and I have been anxiously searching for You."

"Why were you searching for Me?" He asked. "Didn't you know I had to be in My Father's house?"

But they did not understand what He was saying to them.

Then He went down to Nazareth with them and was obedient to them. But His mother treasured all these things in her heart. And Jesus grew in wisdom and stature, and in favor with God and men (Luke 2:41–52).

13. How does Jesus demonstrate His obedience to His Father?

14. "In My Father's house." What blessing have you received from worshiping and studying in God's house?

Forgiven in Christ, we cherish God's Word. Our heavenly Father invites us to worship regularly, to hear His Word preached and taught, and to learn of His grace in Jesus.

God's People Pray

Heavenly Father,
Your Word is our light in life.
Open our hearts daily to Your truth.
Help us to see Your salvation in Christ.
Forgive our sins.
Strengthen our faith.
Send us Your Holy Spirit,
that we may grow in grace and knowledge of Your Word.
To Your glory, through Christ we pray. Amen.

A Verse a Day

Sunday: For where two or three come together in My name, there am I with them. (Matthew 18:20)

Monday: Do not swear falsely by My name and so profane the name of your God. I am the LORD. (Leviticus 19:12)

Tuesday: Call upon Me in the day of trouble; I will deliver you, and you will honor Me. (Psalm 50:15)

Wednesday: For six days, work is to be done, but the seventh day shall be your holy day, a Sabbath of rest to the LORD. Whoever does any work on it must be put to death. (Exodus 35:2)

Thursday: Come to Me, all you who are weary and burdened, and I will give you rest. (Matthew 11:28)

Friday: There remains, then, a Sabbath-rest for the people of God; for anyone who enters God's rest also rests from his own work, just as God did from His. (Hebrews 4:9–10)

Saturday: Let the word of Christ dwell in you richly as you teach and admonish one another with all wisdom, and as you sing psalms, hymns and spiritual songs with gratitude in your hearts to God. (Colossians 3:16)

THE FOURTH *3* COMMANDMENT

Pray Together

Thank You, God,
for all these things that reveal Your love.
Thank You for the heavens that cover us,
for the earth beneath our feet,
for the sun in the day and the stars at night,
for the snow and the rains,
for the mountains and valleys and trees and
    flowers.
Thank You, God,
for those people who demonstrate Your love.
Thank You, God,
for choosing me to be one of Your people,
for calling me and equipping me to communicate
Your love to the world around me.
Thank You, God.

Discover

By His divine power, God rules His creation. In the
Ten Commandments, God forbids us to dishonor His
representatives or to reject their authority. In Christ, our
heavenly Father forgives our failures and helps us to
honor His gifts of authority in our lives.

Introduction

Most nations today have ambassadors. Envoys of the highest rank, ambassadors *represent* their government—the laws, policies, and customs of their nation—to other nations. As the officer in residence, ambassadors are appointed by presidents and rulers and act with full authority.

- Describe how ambassadors benefit our nation and the world.

- In what sense do ambassadors represent the values and principles of their nation?

The Catechism

THE FOURTH COMMANDMENT
Honor your father and your mother.

What does this mean? We should fear and love God so that we do not despise or anger our parents and other authorities, but honor them, serve and obey them, love and cherish them.

Parents and other authorities in our world are God's representatives. They are gifts from God, who act on His behalf to promote peace, stability, and growth in our homes and communities.

In general, authorities include

home: parents, father, mother, or guardians;

school: teachers and administrators;

work: supervisors and managers;

government: elected and appointed officials, national, state, and local law-enforcement agencies, officers, judges, and designated leaders;

church: pastors, DCEs, deaconesses, and other church workers and leaders who serve Christ and His people.

1. In what ways are parents God's representatives in their families?

2. Describe *honor.* How is honor toward parents and other authorities *more than* love?

3. What blessings does God give through authority in our community? in our nation? in our world?

God's Word

At the end of four years, Absalom said to the king [his father David], "Let me go to Hebron and fulfill a vow I made to the LORD. While your servant was living at Geshur in Aram, I made this vow: 'If the LORD takes me back to Jerusalem, I will worship the LORD in Hebron.' "

The king said to him, "Go in peace." So he went to Hebron.

Then Absalom sent secret messengers throughout the tribes of Israel to say, "As soon as you hear the sound of the trumpets, then say, 'Absalom is king in Hebron.' " Two hundred men from Jerusalem had accompanied Absalom. They had been invited as guests and went quite innocently, knowing nothing about the matter. While Absalom was offering sacrifices, he also sent for Ahithophel the Gilonite, David's counselor, to come from Giloh, his hometown. And so the conspiracy gained strength, and Absalom's following kept on increasing.

A messenger came and told David, "The hearts of the men of Israel are with Absalom."

Then David said to all his officials who were with him in Jerusalem, "Come! We must flee, or none of us will escape from Absalom. We must leave immediately, or he will move quickly to overtake us and bring ruin upon us and put the city to the sword."

The king's officials answered him, "Your servants are ready to do whatever our lord the king chooses."

The king set out, with his entire household following him … The whole countryside wept aloud as all the people passed by …

David continued up the Mount of Olives, weeping as he went; his head was covered and he was barefoot. All the people with him covered their heads too and were weeping as they went up …

(2 Samuel 15:7–16, 23, 30).

4. In what ways did Absalom dishonor David as his *father?* as his *king?*

5. How does Absalom's rebellion threaten his *family?* the entire *nation?*

6. In what ways does lack of honor and respect for authority undermine public stability?

God forbids us to dishonor His chosen representatives. Dishonor includes despising, not respecting, and angering parents. It also includes disobeying the lawful authority that parents and others have by God's design. When authority is rejected and undermined, we often suffer the consequences—individually and collectively.

The Family: Foundation

Norbert Oesch writes in *The Ten Commandments,*

> With rare exception, God's authority is channeled through the family. It's like a delta. It springs from this one source, the commandment, into the whole community. That's why we can call our political leaders our civic fathers. It's a family term. The same idea holds true about teachers and employers. Their authority too flows out of the family and ultimately from God. That explains why lawlessness breaks out most openly where the family is weakest or nonexistent.

- What connections do you see between healthy families and healthy communities?

- What happens, in your experience, when authority breaks down in homes? in communities?

God's Word

Joseph went and told Pharaoh, "My father and brothers, with their flocks and herds and everything they own, have come from the land of Canaan and are now in Goshen." He chose five of his brothers and presented them before Pharaoh.

Pharaoh asked the brothers, "What is your occupation?"

"Your servants are shepherds," they replied to Pharaoh, "just as our fathers were." They also said to him, "We have come to live here awhile, because the famine is severe in Canaan and your servants' flocks have no pasture. So now, please let your servants settle in Goshen."

Pharaoh said to Joseph, "Your father and your brothers have come to you, and the land of Egypt is before you; settle your father and your brothers in the best part of the land. Let them live in Goshen. And if you know of any among them with special ability, put them in charge of my own livestock."

Then Joseph brought his father Jacob in and presented him before Pharaoh. After Jacob blessed Pharaoh, Pharaoh asked him, "How old are you?"

And Jacob said to Pharaoh, "The years of my pilgrimage are a hundred and thirty. My years have been few and difficult, and they do not equal the years of the pilgrimage of my fathers."

Then Jacob blessed Pharaoh and went out from his presence.

So Joseph settled his father and his brothers in Egypt and gave them property in the best part of the land, the district of Rameses, as Pharaoh directed. Joseph also provided his father and his brothers and all his father's household with food, according to the number of their children (Genesis 47:1–12).

7. How did Joseph honor his family, especially his father?

8. In what ways was Joseph's family blessed in Egypt?

9. In what ways does God provide for and bless His people through unbelievers?

God gives His mercy and strength to His people. Because of His love in Christ, God forgives our sins and enables us to serve Him by honoring His authority.

Honoring Authority

In his Large Catechism, Martin Luther extends the sphere of God-given authority in our world.

> From the authority of parents all other kinds of authority flow out at various angles …
>
> God provides for us and sustains us through our rulers, as through our parents, with food, house and home, protection and security. And because civil authorities bear the name and title of "parent" as their highest medal of honor, we on our part owe them the honor of thinking highly of them as earth's greatest treasure and most precious jewel.
>
> Yet there is need to impress upon the people that those who want to be known as Christians owe it to God to regard those that watch over their souls as "worthy of double honor" (1 Timothy 5:17), to treat them well, and to provide for their well-being.

10. Why is it difficult to honor government leaders?

11. Describe, as completely as possible, the blessings you have received through good government.

12. In what ways can you show "double honor" to your spiritual leaders—pastors, DCEs, teachers, and other servants of Christ?

God's Word

Everyone must submit himself to the governing authorities, for there is no authority except that which God has established. The authorities that exist have been established by God. Consequently, he who rebels against the authority is rebelling against what God has instituted, and those who do so will bring judgment on themselves. For rulers hold no terror for those who do right, but for those who do wrong. Do you want to be free from fear of the one in authority? Then do what is right and he will commend you. For he is God's servant to do you good. But if you do wrong, be afraid, for he does not bear the sword for nothing. He is God's servant, an agent of wrath to bring punishment on the wrongdoer. Therefore, it is necessary to submit to the authorities, not only because of possible punishment but also because of conscience.

This is also why you pay taxes, for the authorities are God's servants, who give their full time to governing. Give everyone what you owe him: If you owe taxes, pay taxes; if revenue, then revenue; if respect, then respect; if honor, then honor (Romans 13:1–7).

13. What does St. Paul reveal about authority in our world?

14. What does it mean to "submit to the authorities"? Why should God's people submit?

15. How does God's mercy in Christ motivate us to accept and forgive leaders for their failures?

In His death and resurrection, Jesus forgives our sins against the Fourth Commandment. He renews us and gives us His strength to honor parents and authorities as *His* representatives and to serve Him as we serve and obey, love and cherish our leaders.

God's People Pray

Heavenly Father,
keep us under Your care.
In Your goodness, bless our parents.
Bless the leaders of our land,
that we may live in peace
and be a blessing to all nations of the earth.
Give Your wisdom and guidance to all who
serve, protect, and administer justice.
Help us to serve You faithfully in our lives.
To Your glory, through Christ we pray. Amen.

A Verse a Day

Sunday: "Honor your father and mother"—which is the first commandment with a promise—"that it may go well with you and that you may enjoy long life on the earth." (Ephesians 6:2–3)

Monday: Listen to your father, who gave you life, and do not despise your mother when she is old. (Proverbs 23:22)

Tuesday: Children, obey your parents in everything, for this pleases the Lord. (Colossians 3:20)

Wednesday: Remind the people to be subject to rulers and authorities, to be obedient, to be ready to do whatever is good. (Titus 3:1)

Thursday: Rise in the presence of the aged, show respect for the elderly and revere your God. I am the LORD. (Leviticus 19:32)

Friday: Give to Caesar what is Caesar's, and to God what is God's. (Matthew 22:21)

Saturday: Obey your leaders and submit to their authority. They keep watch over you as men who must give an account. Obey them so that their work will be a joy, not a burden, for that would be of no advantage to you. (Hebrews 13:17)

THE FIFTH AND SIXTH COMMANDMENTS

4

Pray Together

O God,
in the grace and strength You grant daily,
I find reason for celebration.
I asked for security,
and You encompassed me with love.
I looked to You for life,
and You granted me life everlasting.
I sought for identity,
and You adopted me as Your child.
Whatever is of value and worth in my life
has come through Your rich blessings.
I find so many reasons for praising You, O God.

Discover

All life is God's gift. In the Ten Commandments, God forbids us to destroy life and relationships in any way. In Christ, our heavenly Father forgives our failures and unfaithfulness and gives us His strength to live as kind, forgiving, and sexually pure children of God.

Introduction

Murder and sex! In many respects, the phrase is a summary of contemporary novels, films, and theater.

Yet art imitates life. Daily headlines chronicle the violence in our communities. Newscasts report sexual scandals and stories of abuse. Though art imitates life, life also creates art.

- In what ways has violence affected your community?

- "Sex. In America an obsession" (Marlene Dietrich). Agree or disagree? Explain your answer.

The Catechism

THE FIFTH COMMANDMENT
You shall not murder.

What does this mean? We should fear and love God so that we do not hurt or harm our neighbor in his body, but help and support him in every physical need.

Most people agree: murder is morally wrong. Yet murder is more than drive-by shootings and premeditated killings. In the Sermon on the Mount, Jesus teaches that murderous acts and intentions all flow from sinful human hearts (Matthew 5:21–22; see also Matthew 15:15–20). In the commandment "You shall not murder," then, God forbids

- taking of human life in all forms: homicide, manslaughter, abortion, euthanasia, and suicide;
- any words and actions that physically harm other people, as well as anything that shortens or makes their life bitter;

35

- constant and deep-seated anger and hatred in our hearts toward other people.

1. What recent headlines in the news relate to the Fifth Commandment?

2. In what ways is hurting or harming another human being an offense to God the Creator?

3. Describe how God's people can "help and support" each other in our physical needs.

God's Word

Adam lay with his wife Eve, and she became pregnant and gave birth to Cain. She said, "With the help of the LORD I have brought forth a man." Later she gave birth to his brother Abel.

Now Abel kept flocks, and Cain worked the soil. In the course of time Cain brought some of the fruits of the soil as an offering to the LORD. But Abel brought fat portions from some of the firstborn of his flock. The LORD looked with favor on Abel and his offering, but on Cain and his offering he did not look with favor. So Cain was very angry, and his face was downcast.

Then the LORD said to Cain, "Why are you angry? Why is your face downcast? If you do what is right, will you not be accepted? But if you do not do what is right, sin is crouching at your door; it desires to have you, but you must master it."

Now Cain said to his brother Abel, "Let's go out to the field." And while they were in the field, Cain attacked his brother Abel and killed him.

Then the L<small>ORD</small> said to Cain, "Where is your brother Abel?"

"I don't know," he replied. "Am I my brother's keeper?"

The L<small>ORD</small> said, "What have you done? Listen! Your brother's blood cries out to Me from the ground. Now you are under a curse and driven from the ground, which opened its mouth to receive your brother's blood from your hand. When you work the ground, it will no longer yield its crops for you. You will be a restless wanderer on the earth."

Cain said to the L<small>ORD</small>, "My punishment is more than I can bear. Today You are driving me from the land, and I will be hidden from Your presence; I will be a restless wanderer on the earth, and whoever finds me will kill me."

But the L<small>ORD</small> said to him, "Not so; if anyone kills Cain, he will suffer vengeance seven times over." Then the L<small>ORD</small> put a mark on Cain so that no one who found him would kill him. So Cain went out from the L<small>ORD</small>'s presence and lived in the land of Nod, east of Eden (Genesis 4:1–16).

4. What motivated Cain to kill his brother?

5. "Am I my brother's keeper?" In what ways is Cain's response a universal human excuse?

6. How does God demonstrate His grace in the account of Cain and Abel?

Murder is wrong! Murder, in all its forms, is an affront—a sin—against the God who created life. From gang revenge to killing the unborn or the elderly, murder is forbidden in God's holy Word. Moreover, God forbids us to hurt or harm our neighbor through our attitudes and behavior.

No one has kept the Fifth Commandment—except Jesus. In His ministry Jesus demonstrated the kindness and compassion of God to all people. Though innocent, He was killed—murdered on the cross—for our forgiveness and life.

God's Word

[The expert in the law] asked Jesus, "And who is my neighbor?"

In reply Jesus said: "A man was going down from Jerusalem to Jericho, when he fell into the hands of robbers. They stripped him of his clothes, beat him and went away, leaving him half dead. A priest happened to be going down the same road, and when he saw the man, he passed by on the other side. So too, a Levite, when he came to the place and saw him, passed by on the other side. But a Samaritan, as he traveled, came where the man was; and when he saw him, he took pity on him. He went to him and bandaged his wounds, pouring on oil and wine. Then he put the man on his own donkey, took him to an inn and took care of him. The next day he took out two silver coins and gave them to the innkeeper. 'Look after him,' he said, 'and when I return, I will reimburse you for any extra expense you may have.'

"Which of these three do you think was a neighbor to the man who fell into the hands of robbers?"

The expert in the law replied, "The one who had mercy on him."

Jesus told him, "Go and do likewise" (Luke 10:29–37).

7. In what ways did the priest and Levite "hurt and harm" the beaten man?

8. How did the Samaritan "help and support" the beaten man?

9. How does the "Good Samaritan" remind you of Jesus?

"Go and do likewise." On our own, we cannot do what God requires. But in Christ, we want to—and with His strength can—help and support our "neighbors." We want to, as Rudolph Norden writes in *With Jesus Every Day*,

> Because our Savior, Jesus Christ, chose to become involved in our behalf. He did for us in a spiritual sense what the Good Samaritan did for his victim: He took proper measures to heal us from the wounds of sin, save us from death, and make us well. We cannot repay Jesus for this, but we can show our thankfulness by helping others in need.

The Catechism

The Sixth Commandment
You shall not commit adultery.

What does this mean? We should fear and love God so that we lead a sexually pure and decent life in what we say and do, and husband and wife love and honor each other.

In a time and place of diverse views on sexuality, God's Word offers trustworthy absolutes. A sexually pure and decent life means we regard sexuality as God's good gift to His creation;

we honor marriage—one man and one woman—as instituted and blessed by God;

we engage in acts of sexual intimacy only with our spouse;

we control our sex drive in ways that please God.

10. Is it more difficult today to live a "sexually pure and decent life"? Explain your answer.

11. What temptations do God's people face in relation to their sexuality?

12. Describe, as completely as possible, love and honor in a marriage relationship.

God's Word

The LORD God said, "It is not good for the man to be alone. I will make a helper suitable for him."

Now the LORD God had formed out of the ground all the beasts of the field and all the birds of the air. He brought them to the man to see what he would name them; and whatever the man called each living creature, that was its name. So the man gave names to all the livestock, the birds of the air and all the beasts of the field. But for Adam no suitable helper was found.

So the LORD God caused the man to fall into a deep sleep; and while he was sleeping, He took one of the man's ribs and closed up the place with flesh. Then the LORD God made a woman from the rib He had taken out of the man, and He brought her to the man.

The man said,

"This is now bone of my bones and flesh of my flesh;
she shall be called 'woman,' for she was taken out of man."

For this reason a man will leave his father and mother and be united to his wife, and they will become one flesh.
The man and his wife were both naked, and they felt no shame (Genesis 2:18–25).

13. How does God's Word reveal the *inter*dependence of male and female, husband and wife?

14. What blessings has God given to our world through marriage? through singleness?

Adultery, divorce, sexual immorality, and indecency are part of our fallen world. Yet God forgives *all* sexual sin in Christ. Because of Jesus' death and resurrection we have new life; we can, by the power of God's Spirit, avoid temptation and use our sexuality to honor and glorify God.

God's People Pray

Heavenly Father, God of all grace,
we thank You for Your gift of life.
Keep us in Your care and protection.
Defend us against all harm and danger.
Bless our homes with Your love and faithfulness.
Help us to live together in peace,
that we may witness to Your Son, our Savior.
To Your glory, through Christ we pray. Amen.

A Verse a Day

Sunday: Your eyes saw my unformed body. All the days ordained for me were written in Your book before one of them came to be. (Psalm 139:16)

Monday: Speak up for those who cannot speak for themselves, for the rights of all who are destitute. (Proverbs 31:8)

Tuesday: Do not take revenge, my friends, but leave room for God's wrath, for it is written: "It is mine to avenge; I will repay," says the Lord. (Romans 12:19)

Wednesday: "In your anger do not sin": Do not let the sun go down while you are still angry. (Ephesians 4:26)

Thursday: Marriage should be honored by all, and the marriage bed kept pure, for God will judge the adulterer and all the sexually immoral. (Hebrews 13:4)

Friday: So they are no longer two, but one. Therefore what God has joined together, let man not separate. (Matthew 19:6)

Saturday: Do you not know that your body is a temple of the Holy Spirit, who is in you, whom you have received from God? You are not your own; you were bought at a price. Therefore honor God with your body. (1 Corinthians 6:19–20)

THE SEVENTH AND EIGHTH COMMANDMENTS

5

Pray Together

My heart bursts with praises to God;
every fiber of my being reaches out in rejoicing!
How can I ever forget His many blessings?
He forgives all my sins;
He touches my afflictions with healing;
He snatches me back from the gaping jaws of hell;
He covers me with concern and love;
He fulfills my deepest desires and gives me
meaning for life and purpose for living.
Whoever and wherever you are,
lift your hearts in praise to God.

Discover

God gives us possessions and our reputation. In the Ten Commandments, God forbids us to steal or to give false testimony. In Christ, our heavenly Father forgives our sins against His Word and helps us to live honestly and honorably with all people.

43

Introduction

A story from ancient times is told about Diogenes, a Greek philosopher who fashioned himself a "watchdog" of contemporary morals. In a stinging indictment of his fellow citizens, Diogenes began a search, in broad daylight with a lighted lantern, for "honest people."

He found none.

- In what ways is honesty a rare trait in our world?

- "Honesty is the best policy." Why is honesty difficult in business? in politics? in our families?

The Catechism

THE SEVENTH COMMANDMENT
You shall not steal.

What does this mean? We should fear and love God so that we do not take our neighbor's money or possessions, or get them in any dishonest way, but help him to improve and protect his possessions and income.

Stealing is common. For some people, stealing is a "minor matter," an insignificant concern among the many other social problems. "Nobody gets hurt in shoplifting." "Everybody cheats on taxes." "The restaurant will never miss the extra 10 dollars."

In the Seventh Commandment, God forbids every kind of stealing, including robbery, theft, and dishonest ways of acquiring possessions.

1. What specific kinds of actions fall under *stealing*?

2. What, at root, does stealing reveal about human hearts?

3. In what ways can we "improve and protect" our neighbor's "possessions and income"?

God's Word

Jesus entered Jericho and was passing through. A man was there by the name of Zacchaeus; he was a chief tax collector and was wealthy. He wanted to see who Jesus was, but being a short man he could not, because of the crowd. So he ran ahead and climbed a sycamore-fig tree to see him, since Jesus was coming that way.

When Jesus reached the spot, He looked up and said to him, "Zacchaeus, come down immediately. I must stay at your house today." So he came down at once and welcomed Him gladly.

All the people saw this and began to mutter, "He has gone to be the guest of a 'sinner.'"

But Zacchaeus stood up and said to the Lord, "Look, Lord! Here and now I give half of my possessions to the poor, and if I have cheated anybody out of anything, I will pay back four times the amount."

Jesus said to him, "Today salvation has come to this house, because this man, too, is a son of Abraham. For the Son of Man came to seek and to save what was lost" (Luke 19:1–10).

4. What attitudes and feelings would people have held toward Zacchaeus? would Zacchaeus have held toward the people?

5. In what ways does Jesus change Zacchaeus?

6. What does it mean that Jesus came "to seek and to save what was lost"?

Through Christ and His strength, we can serve others by respecting and protecting their possessions, by improving and enriching their lives, and by sharing our blessings.

The Catechism

THE EIGHTH COMMANDMENT
You shall not give false testimony against your neighbor.

What does this mean? We should fear and love God so that we do not tell lies about our neighbor, betray him, slander him, or hurt his reputation, but defend him, speak well of him, and explain everything in the kindest way.

In *Keeping the Faith* (St. Louis: Concordia, 1997), Terry K. Dittmer writes,

The Eighth Commandment is about telling the truth. It's about reputations and what we say about other people. The Eighth Commandment is also about how we use language. What we say about someone may ruin their reputation. What we say may also help to build another's reputation.
The Eighth Commandment is about minding our tongue and being careful about what we say about each other.

7. How do false testimony, lies, and slander destroy lives? destroy societies?

8. In what ways is the Eighth Commandment important in a positive Christian witness?

9. "Explain everything in the kindest way." What blessings come from putting the "best construction" on actions at work? in our family?

God's Word

Now a man named Ananias, together with his wife Sapphira, also sold a piece of property. With his wife's full knowledge he kept back part of the money for himself, but brought the rest and put it at the apostles' feet.

Then Peter said, "Ananias, how is it that Satan has so filled your heart that you have lied to the Holy Spirit and have kept for yourself some of the money you received for the land? Didn't it belong to you before it was sold? And after it was sold, wasn't the money at your disposal? What made you think of doing such a thing? You have not lied to men but to God."

When Ananias heard this, he fell down and died. And great fear seized all who heard what had happened. Then the young men came forward, wrapped up his body, and carried him out and buried him.

About three hours later his wife came in, not knowing what had happened. Peter asked her, "Tell me, is this the price you and Ananias got for the land?"

"Yes," she said, "that is the price."

Peter said to her, "How could you agree to test the Spirit of the Lord? Look! The feet of the men who buried your husband are at the door, and they will carry you out also."

At that moment she fell down at his feet and died. Then the young men came in and, finding her dead, carried her out and buried her beside her husband. Great fear seized the whole church and all who heard about these events (Acts 5:1–11).

10. In what ways did Ananias lie? In what ways did Sapphira lie?

11. How did their false testimony threaten the believers' fellowship in the church?

12. In what ways are honesty and truthfulness vital characteristics of life together in the body of Christ?

God forbids us to tell lies in a court of law, in the workplace, at home, and everywhere. We sin against His will when we speak words that betray someone (break a trust), slander someone, or damage another person's reputation.

Though we are all guilty of breaking the Eighth Commandment, God gives us His grace in Christ. Jesus' death and resurrection are our forgiveness. By the power of His Spirit alive in us, we can

- defend our neighbor from all false allegations;

- speak well of others;

- explain their actions in the best possible way.

God's People Pray

Heavenly Father,
You have given us all things in Your goodness.
Help us to remember and give thanks for our
    blessings.
Strengthen us to do Your will.
Bless our land, our homes, our work.
Save us from violence, discord, and danger.
Let Your wisdom and truth shine in our lives,
that all people may know Your power and grace.
To Your glory, through Christ we pray. Amen.

A Verse a Day

Sunday: So in everything, do to others what you would have them do to you, for this sums up the Law and the Prophets. (Matthew 7:12)

Monday: He who has been stealing must steal no longer, but must work, doing something useful with his own hands, that he may have something to share with those in need. (Ephesians 4:28)

Tuesday: And do not forget to do good and to share with others, for with such sacrifices God is pleased. (Hebrews 13:16)

Wednesday: Therefore each of you must put off falsehood and speak truthfully to his neighbor, for we are all members of one body. (Ephesians 4:25)

Thursday: A gossip betrays a confidence, but a trustworthy man keeps a secret. (Proverbs 11:13)

Friday: Do not judge, and you will not be judged. Do not condemn, and you will not be condemned. Forgive, and you will be forgiven. (Luke 6:37)

Saturday: Above all, love each other deeply, because love covers over a multitude of sins. (1 Peter 4:8)

THE NINTH AND TENTH COMMANDMENTS 6

Pray Together

The Lord is my constant companion.
There is no need that He cannot fulfill.
Whether His course for me points
to the mountaintops of glorious joy
or to the valleys of human suffering,
He is by my side.
He is ever present with me.
My security is in His promise
to be near me always
and in the knowledge
that He will never let me go.

Discover

God wants His people to be content. In the Ten Commandments, God forbids us to covet anything that belongs to our neighbor. In Christ, our heavenly Father forgives our sinful desires and actions and enables us to live as His grateful, joyful people.

Introduction

In many parts of our world and nation, the key word is *simplicity:* simple lifestyles, simple needs and

wants, simple pleasures in work and relationships.
　　"All the loveliest things there be
　　Come simply, so, it seems to me."
　　(Edna St. Vincent Millay)

- What do you appreciate about simplicity?

- In your experience, in what ways can simplicity lead to contentment?

The Catechism

THE NINTH COMMANDMENT
You shall not covet your neighbor's house.

What does this mean? We should fear and love God so that we do not scheme to get our neighbor's inheritance or house, or get it in a way which only appears right, but help and be of service to him in keeping it.

In the last two commandments, the word *covet* refers to sinful desires for anyone or anything that "belongs" to another person. *Covetousness* is misdirected desire; it focuses on what is rightfully—morally and legally—not ours. It is, of course, not wrong or sinful to want a new car. It is, however, wrong and sinful to want our neighbor's new car. To covet in our hearts often leads to hurtful actions toward others.

1. "Covetousness is simply craving more of what you have enough of already" (H. Robinson). Agree or disagree? Share your response.

2. The Ninth Commandment centers on property: "your neighbor's house." In what ways is your home or farm part of who you are?

3. How can we help others to "keep" their house and property?

God forbids us to covet another's property or to make plans to acquire it in an open or deceptive way.

God's Word

Some time later there was an incident involving a vineyard belonging to Naboth the Jezreelite. The vineyard was in Jezreel, close to the palace of Ahab king of Samaria. Ahab said to Naboth, "Let me have your vineyard to use for a vegetable garden, since it is close to my palace. In exchange I will give you a better vineyard or, if you prefer, I will pay you whatever it is worth."

But Naboth replied, "The LORD forbid that I should give you the inheritance of my fathers."

So Ahab went home, sullen and angry because Naboth the Jezreelite had said, "I will not give you the inheritance of my fathers." He lay on his bed sulking and refused to eat.

His wife Jezebel came in and asked him, "Why are you so sullen? Why won't you eat?"

He answered her, "Because I said to Naboth the Jezreelite, 'Sell me your vineyard; or if you prefer, I will give you another vineyard in its place.' But he said, 'I will not give you my vineyard.' "

Jezebel his wife said, "Is this how you act as king over Israel? Get up and eat! Cheer up. I'll get you the vineyard of Naboth the Jezreelite."

So she wrote letters in Ahab's name, placed his seal

on them, and sent them to the elders and nobles who lived in Naboth's city with him.

In those letters she wrote: "Proclaim a day of fasting and seat Naboth in a prominent place among the people.

"But seat two scoundrels opposite him and have them testify that he has cursed both God and the king. Then take him out and stone him to death."

So the elders and nobles who lived in Naboth's city did as Jezebel directed in the letters she had written to them. They proclaimed a fast and seated Naboth in a prominent place among the people. Then two scoundrels came and sat opposite him and brought charges against Naboth before the people, saying, "Naboth has cursed both God and the king." So they took him outside the city and stoned him to death. Then they sent word to Jezebel: "Naboth has been stoned and is dead."

As soon as Jezebel heard that Naboth had been stoned to death, she said to Ahab, "Get up and take possession of the vineyard of Naboth the Jezreelite that he refused to sell you. He is no longer alive, but dead." When Ahab heard that Naboth was dead, he got up and went down to take possession of Naboth's vineyard (1 Kings 21:1–16).

4. What are Ahab's and Jezebel's sins? How were their actions the result of sinful desires?

5. In what ways did their sins affect Naboth's family? the larger community?

6. How does covetousness in our day hurt society as a whole?

A favorite Christian hymn notes,
We give You but Your own, In any gifts we bring;
All that we have is Yours alone, A trust from You, our King.

Because God gives us all that we have, He calls us to be thankful and to live in contentment. God wants His people to serve others with the gifts He has entrusted to our care.

The Catechism

THE TENTH COMMANDMENT

You shall not covet your neighbor's wife, or his manservant or maidservant, his ox or donkey, or anything that belongs to your neighbor.

What does this mean? We should fear and love God so that we do not entice or force away our neighbor's wife, workers, or animals, or turn them against him, but urge them to stay and do their duty.

Nobert Oesch writes in *The Ten Commandments*,

Is coveting a serious sin? It is even worse than we would first imagine. In the Old Testament Job tells us a very revealing thing: "If I had put my trust in gold, … then these also would be sins to be judged, for I would have been unfaithful to God on high" (Job 31:24, 28).

Coveting is *not* such a small thing. It is an idolatry that replaces God and encourages us to treat other people as less than human, as less than the special creations of God they are.

54

7. In what ways is coveting like idolatry—putting something else before God?

8. The Tenth Commandment centers on people and livelihood: spouse, workers, farm animals, etc. In what ways does family and career define who we are in life?

9. How can we encourage others to be faithful in their relationships and callings?

A Christian teacher once remarked, "Next to faith this is the highest art—to be content with the calling in which God has placed you. I have not learned it yet."

Because of sin, we are often restless and unsatisfied in life. Yet Christ forgives our sinful desires and deeds. He renews us with His mercy and love. He strengthens us to live in love toward all people.

God's Word

As Jesus started on His way, a man ran up to Him and fell on his knees before Him. "Good teacher," he asked, "what must I do to inherit eternal life?"

"Why do you call Me good?" Jesus answered. "No one is good—except God alone. You know the commandments: 'Do not murder, do not commit adultery, do not steal, do not give false testimony, do not defraud, honor your father and mother.' "

"Teacher," he declared, "all these I have kept since I was a boy."

Jesus looked at him and loved him. "One thing you

lack," He said. "Go, sell everything you have and give to the poor, and you will have treasure in heaven. Then come, follow Me."

At this the man's face fell. He went away sad, because he had great wealth.

Jesus looked around and said to His disciples, "How hard it is for the rich to enter the kingdom of God!"

The disciples were amazed at His words. But Jesus said again, "Children, how hard it is to enter the kingdom of God! It is easier for a camel to go through the eye of a needle than for a rich man to enter the kingdom of God."

The disciples were even more amazed, and said to each other, "Who then can be saved?"

Jesus looked at them and said, "With man this is impossible, but not with God; all things are possible with God" (Mark 10:17–27).

10. Describe the man's attitude toward his life and toward his wealth.

11. What does Jesus' response, "Go, sell everything ... Then come, follow Me," reveal about God's kingdom?

12. What comfort do you have in knowing all things—including our salvation—are "possible with God"?

Each commandment confronts us with the question, "Have I kept God's Law? Have I obeyed His Word in all my thoughts, my words, and my actions?"

Our answer is clearly no.

God gave His Law for three purposes:

As a curb, to keep order in the world and control flagrant sinfulness

As a mirror, to enable us to see our sins and failures as well as our need

As a guide, to show how God intends His forgiven people to live for Him

The Law, then, points us to Christ, the world's one Savior. Jesus fulfilled God's Law perfectly in His life, and in His death He suffered the punishment for our disobedience to God's Word. In His resurrection He defeated sin, death, and Satan and now pours out His forgiveness, life, and salvation through the Gospel.

In Christ alone, we have the power to seek God's will in our lives. Through Christ, God's Word in His commandments is "a lamp to my feet, and a light for my path" (Psalm 119:105).

God's People Pray

Almighty and everlasting God,
> in Jesus You have forgiven our sins
> and given Your rich blessings for our life.
Send us Your Holy Spirit.
Rule in our hearts through Your grace.
Keep us in Your Fatherly care.
Help us to overcome the world,
> and serve You as Your holy people.
All thanks and praise to You, loving Father.
To Your glory, through Christ we pray. Amen.

A Verse a Day

Sunday: I am not saying this because I am in need, for I have learned to be content whatever the circumstances. (Philippians 4:11)

Monday: But godliness with contentment is great gain. (1 Timothy 6:6)

Tuesday: Keep your lives free from the love of money and be content with what you have, because God has said, "Never will I leave you; never will I forsake you." (Hebrews 13:5)

Wednesday: [Jesus] said to them, "Watch out! Be on your guard against all kinds of greed; a man's life does not consist in the abundance of his possessions." (Luke 12:15)

Thursday: Put to death, therefore, whatever belongs to your earthly nature: sexual immorality, impurity, lust, evil desires and greed, which is idolatry. (Colossians 3:5)

Friday: Delight yourself in the LORD and He will give you the desires of your heart. (Psalm 37:4)

Saturday: Finally, brothers, whatever is true, whatever is noble, whatever is right, whatever is pure, whatever is lovely, whatever is admirable—if anything is excellent or praiseworthy—think about such things. (Philippians 4:8)

LEADERS NOTES

The format for each session is similar. For notes on how to guide participants through the parts of the Study Guide, see session 1.

As you prepare to lead the session,

- read the Study Guide and answer the questions as fully as possible.

As you prepare for your time together,

- arrive early to make sure the setting is comfortable.
- greet participants by name.
- introduce participants to one another.
- thank participants for their time and commitment.
- keep in mind that sometimes participants may be reluctant to share their thoughts about some issues. Help participants see that God's solid Word guides us as we apply Law and Gospel to our lives. In Christian love we can discuss difficult issues, even though at times we may differ on how God's Word can be applied to our lives.

1 THE FIRST COMMANDMENT AND THE CONCLUSION TO THE COMMANDMENTS

Pray Together

Use the prayer as you begin the session.

Discover

Read aloud the session theme.

Introduction

Read aloud, or invite a participant to read aloud, the brief introduction to the session. In general, spend 5–10 minutes on the Introduction questions.

Allow participants to write down and share aloud their questions.

- Answers will vary but may include financial security, career, sports, family, etc.
- Answers will vary. Encourage participant discussion.

Read the introductory paragraph on the Ten Commandments as God's Law.

The Catechism

Read the First Commandment and Luther's explanation from the Small Catechism. Read aloud, or invite a volunteer to read aloud, the paragraphs and questions on the meaning of the commandment.

Invite participants to share their responses.

1. Fear is reverence, respect, awe, admiration, and a proper sense of the majesty, glory, and righteousness of God. Love means to cherish, to cling to God, to devote our lives to Him, and to regard God as our dear Father. Trust is faith in the heart, commitment to God as Lord and Savior, and reliance on Him for our needs.

2. Answers may vary but will likely include the responses mentioned in the Introduction under "main thing."

3. To cling to God is to hold on to His Word, His will, and His ways, to adhere to His message of love and forgiveness in Christ, and to cherish with our whole heart His goodness to us.

God's Word

Invite a participant to read aloud this portion from Holy Scripture. Use the questions for reflection and discussion on the text.

4. Encourage participant discussion. People today are like the people of Israel in our natural tendency to idolatry, our quick abandonment of God's will, our forgetfulness toward God's goodness and mercy, etc.

5. Answers will vary but may include the sinful desire for new experiences, new "types" of satisfaction, or new patterns of worship.

6. The story of the golden calf reveals God's contempt for idols and His righteous anger toward idolatry. Yet God is always merciful and seeks to spare and save His people because of His great love in Christ.

Read aloud the paragraphs on idolatry and God's forgiveness in Jesus. As possible, encourage participants to discuss the bullet questions.

- The main thing for Christians is their relationship to the triune God through Baptism and faith. Allow participants to share how their faith impacts their daily life.
- Encourage responses on how faith in Christ shapes their attitudes, priorities, work habits, etc.

God's Word

Invite a participant to read aloud this portion from Holy Scripture. Use the questions for reflection and discussion on the text.

7. Allow participants to express their thoughts and feelings on the remarkable story of Abraham and Isaac. Responses may include fear, brokenness, faith, assurance, or comfort in the midst of death. If time permits, share Hebrews 11:17–19:

> By faith Abraham, when God tested him, offered Isaac as a sacrifice. He who had received the promises was about to sacrifice his one and only son, even though God had said to him, "It is through Isaac that your offspring will be reckoned." Abraham reasoned that God could raise the dead, and figuratively speaking, he did receive Isaac back from death.

8. Abraham demonstrates his complete trust in God by hearing God's command, believing God, trusting Him in the midst of an uncertain outcome, and obeying His Word.

9. Allow participants to reflect on the ways that the story reminds us of God's sacrifice of His Son for the sins of the world. Like Isaac, Jesus goes willingly, at His Father's desire, to the place of sacrifice. Unlike Isaac, however, Jesus died to win forgiveness, life, and salvation for fallen, sinful human beings.

The Catechism

Invite a participant to read The Close of the Commandments and Luther's explanation. Then allow participants to reflect on and answer the questions.

10. Answers will vary, but may refer to opinions that the commandments are no longer binding or relevant for our modern day.

11. Encourage participants to share how Jesus' forgiveness gives encouragement and strength in the midst of life's many failures and hardships.

12. Encourage participant responses.

God's People Pray

Use the prayer as a closing devotion. If you wish, include special prayers for needs of participants, your congregation, your community, the nation or world.

A Verse a Day

Encourage participants to read and memorize the Bible verse for each day.

2 THE SECOND AND THIRD COMMANDMENTS

Pray Together

Use the prayer as you begin the session.

Discover

Read aloud the session theme.

Introduction

Read aloud, or invite a participant to read aloud, the brief introduction to the session.

- Answers will vary but may include that our words tell about our background, priorities, religious beliefs, values, etc.
- Answers will vary. Encourage participant discussion on the ways books, movies, and television shape our identity and behavior.

The Catechism

Read the Second Commandment and Luther's explanation from the Small Catechism. Read aloud, or invite a volunteer to read aloud, the paragraphs and questions on the meaning of the commandment.

Invite participants to share their responses.

1. Accept participant responses. Answers may include cursing by God's name, profanity, swearing, etc.

Encourage participants to identify specific situations where people misuse God's name.

2. Allow participants to share times when they have called on God's name in their times of trouble and times of praise and thanksgiving.

3. Encourage participants to share their encouragement in knowing Jesus as Lord and Savior.

God's Word

Invite a participant to read aloud this portion from Holy Scripture. Use the questions for reflection and discussion on the text.

4. In the burning bush, God reveals that He is the all-powerful God, the holy and eternal God, who is the God of Abraham, Isaac, and Jacob. He is, therefore, the creator of the universe and the Lord who called His people into existence through Abraham. In the name I AM WHO I AM, God reveals Himself as the eternal God, the One from everlasting to everlasting, who is beyond human understanding and strength.

5. Moses took off his shoes in the presence of God and hid his face, because he was overwhelmed by the glory and power of God.

6. Accept participant responses. Like God's promise to Moses, "I will be with you," God speaks His promise to us: "I am with you always" (Matthew 28:20). For our small and large tasks, God gives His grace and strength.

God's Word

Invite a participant to read aloud this portion from Holy Scripture. Use the questions for reflection and discussion on the text.

7. The lepers would have faced the hardship of physical pain, poverty, isolation, and perhaps public scorn. For these partners in suffering, life *was* difficult.

8. The nine lepers, although perhaps grateful, have no time or inclination to return to Jesus and express their thanks. The one leper demonstrates his gratitude by

returning to Jesus, falling at His feet, and thanking Him.

9. Accept participant responses. Jesus forgives us and, according to His purpose, heals and provides for us so that we may serve Him. Through faith, we receive His blessings of life and salvation.

The Catechism

Invite a participant to read the Third Commandment and Luther's explanation and the paragraphs on the Sabbath. Then allow participants to reflect on and answer the questions.

10. Allow participants to share how attitudes toward Sunday as the Lord's Day have changed, e.g., in family plans, store hours, more emphasis on recreation, less on rest and worship, etc.

11. God's people sin against the Third Commandment when they neglect worship, refuse to hear and study God's Word, attend church reluctantly, and in general when they fail to recognize God's gifts in the day of worship.

12. A regular day of rest—Sunday—provides our bodies with needed rest. Regularly, weekly worship brings us God's Word and sacraments to strengthen our faith and draw us closer to our Savior Jesus Christ.

God's Word

Invite a participant to read aloud this portion from Holy Scripture. Use the questions for reflection and discussion on the text.

13. Jesus demonstrated His obedience to His Father as He heard God's Word taught in the temple, as He devoted Himself to His Father's ways, and as He modeled His reverence for God's house.

14. Encourage participants to share the joy, peace, and other blessings they have as they gather with friends and fellow believers in weekly worship and study.

God's People Pray

Use the prayer as a closing devotion. If you wish, include special prayers for needs of participants, your congregation, your community, the nation or world.

A Verse a Day

Encourage participants to read and memorize the Bible verse for each day.

3 THE FOURTH COMMANDMENT

Pray Together

Use the prayer as you begin the session.

Discover

Read aloud the session theme.

Introduction

Read aloud, or invite a participant to read aloud, the brief introduction to the session.

- Answers will vary but may include fostering peace and goodwill among nations, combatting international crime, helping trade arrangements, etc.
- Answers will vary. Encourage participant discussion.

The Catechism

Read the Fourth Commandment and Luther's explanation from the Small Catechism. Read aloud, or invite a volunteer to read aloud, the paragraphs and questions on the meaning of the commandment.

Invite participants to share their responses.

1. Parents are called by God to represent His authority, will, and love in their families. They have been given a sacred trust in children, and God calls them to teach their children His Word.

2. Honor includes respect, esteem, and regard for one's position. Honor is not given on the basis of what one does, but rather who one is. Honor is more than feelings of affection; it is proper respect for what one represents.

3. Answers will vary, but may include stability, peace, order, prosperity, education, commerce, industry, safe streets, global cooperation, etc.

God's Word

Invite a participant to read aloud this portion from Holy Scripture. Use the questions for reflection and discussion on the text.

4. Absalom dishonored David as his father by trying to take David's rightful place in the family and by speaking falsely about David. Absalom dishonored David as king by claiming in effect that David was a poor judge and that Absalom would make a better king.

5. Absalom's rebellion threatened to break down David's entire family by creating a crisis in parental authority. The rebellion also threatened the entire nation by creating a crisis in the law and the governance of the people.

6. Lack of honor and respect undermines public stability by creating dissension, gridlock, hatred, and other forms of discord.

The Family: Foundation

Invite a volunteer to read aloud the paragraphs on the family as the channel of God's authority in the world. Then ask participants to reflect on and answer the bullet questions.

- Answers will vary on the connections between healthy families and healthy communities but may include safe, stable neighborhoods, good schools, low crime rates, etc.
- Accept participant responses.

God's Word

Invite a participant to read aloud this portion from Holy Scripture. Use the questions for reflection and discussion on the text.

7. Joseph honored his father by welcoming him to Egypt and presenting him to Pharoah—an extraordinary privilege in the ancient world! He also honored his father by showing great kindness to his brothers, his father's sons.

8. Joseph's family was blessed with a good place to live and a livelihood. Joseph arranged the details, but all the blessings came from God.

9. God provides for and blesses His people through unbelievers in good government, technology, medicine, business, agriculture, etc.

Honoring Authority

Invite a participant to read the paragraphs on authority in the world. Then allow participants to reflect on and answer the questions.

10. Accept participant responses. Answers may include differing political views, differing views on policy, reputations, past actions, etc.

11. Encourage participants to share the blessings they have received through good, stable government.

12. Again, encourage participants to reflect on and suggest ways that they can honor their spiritual leaders, as Luther notes in his Large Catechism.

God's Word

Invite a participant to read aloud this portion from Holy Scripture. Use the questions for reflection and discussion on the text.

13. Authority is God's gift to the world; all authority exists by His will and establishment. Unlawful rebellion against government is a sin against God's will.

14. To submit is to honor and respect authorities, obey the laws of the land and decisions of the courts,

and to live with integrity in our speech and actions. God's people submit in order to honor God and His Word. When nations make laws and rulings that violate or contradict God's Law, God's people are called to obey God, not human authorities.

15. Encourage participants to respond to Christ's forgiveness in our lives and our forgiveness of others, including political and spiritual leaders.

God's People Pray

Use the prayer as a closing devotion. If you wish, include special prayers for needs of participants, your congregation, your community, the nation or world.

A Verse a Day

Encourage participants to read and memorize the Bible verse for each day.

4 THE FIFTH AND SIXTH COMMANDMENTS

Pray Together

Use the prayer as you begin the session.

Discover

Read aloud the session theme.

Introduction

Read aloud, or invite a participant to read aloud, the brief introduction to the session.

- Answers will vary but may include murder, rape, abuse, and other violent crimes and actions, both in "real life" and in the media.
- Answers may vary. Encourage participant discussion but be sensitive to differing viewpoints.

The Catechism

Read the Fifth Commandment and Luther's explanation from the Small Catechism. Read aloud, or invite a volunteer to read aloud, the paragraphs and questions on the meaning of the commandment.

Invite participants to share their responses.

1. Accept participant responses. Answers may—and should be—broader than murder.

2. Any word or action that hurts or harms another person is a sin against God, for God is creator of all and

His creatures are called to live in peace with one another. If time permits, share James 3:9–10: "With the tongue we praise our Lord and Father, and with it we curse men, who have been made in God's likeness. Out of the same mouth come praise and cursing. My brothers, this should not be." God's Law applies to both our speech and actions.

3. Answers will vary. Encourage participant discussion.

God's Word

Invite a participant to read aloud this portion from Holy Scripture. Use the questions for reflection and discussion on the text.

4. Cain was angry at God, at his brother, and likely at himself. His anger blinded him to God's forgiveness.

5. Accept participant responses. In one sense, all people, by nature, excuse themselves from caring for other human beings.

6. God's patient and steadfast love offered Cain an opportunity to live and repent. In Christ, God offers His grace to all—even to the worst murderers.

God's Word

Invite a participant to read aloud this portion from Holy Scripture. Use the questions for reflection and discussion on the text.

7. The priest and Levite hurt and harmed the beaten man by ignoring and neglecting his needs.

8. The Samaritan, in contrast, helped and supported the beaten man by bandaging his wounds, transporting the man to an inn, and providing for his recovery.

9. The Good Samaritan is a picture of Christ, the compassionate Savior who rescues, heals, and restores His people.

The Catechism

Invite a participant to read the Sixth Commandment

and Luther's explanation. Then allow participants to reflect on and answer the questions.

10. Accept participant responses. Some may affirm that it is more difficult to live a sexually pure and decent life today because of the many forms of sexuality expressed in media, books, etc.

11. Allow participants to share the temptations they face in life.

12. Encourage participant responses. Answers may include caring words and acts, special gifts at appropriate times, living in forgiveness, affirming each other in front of children and friends, etc.

God's Word

Invite a participant to read aloud this portion from Holy Scripture. Use the questions for reflection and discussion on the text.

13. In Genesis, God reveals that male and female, husband and wife, are interdependent, both in their creation and in their purpose in life. Allow participants to explore this beautiful passage.

14. Accept participant responses on both issues. Affirm that God blesses His world and His church through both marriage and singleness.

God's People Pray

Use the prayer as a closing devotion. If you wish, include special prayers for needs of participants, your congregation, your community, the nation or world.

A Verse a Day

Encourage participants to read and memorize the Bible verse for each day.

5 THE SEVENTH AND EIGHTH COMMANDMENTS

Pray Together

Use the prayer as you begin the session.

Discover

Read aloud the session theme.

Introduction

Read aloud, or invite a participant to read aloud, the brief introduction to the session.

- Answers will vary but may include references to the frequent scandals in politics, business, entertainment, as well as the pressures we face to be successful in all situations.
- Answers will vary. Encourage participant discussion.

The Catechism

Read the Seventh Commandment and Luther's explanation from the Small Catechism. Read aloud, or invite a volunteer to read aloud, the paragraphs and questions on the meaning of the commandment.

Invite participants to share their responses.

1. Allow participants to suggest specific kinds of actions that can be labeled stealing: e.g., embezzlement, fraud, shoplifting, carjacking, etc.

2. Stealing reveals that human beings are not grateful for what they have; stealing also shows desperation in the heart and the fear that God will not provide for our needs.

3. Accept participant responses.

God's Word

Invite a participant to read aloud this portion from Holy Scripture. Use the questions for reflection and discussion on the text.

4. Many people would have resented Zacchaeus; as a tax collector, Zacchaeus would likely have intimidated and oppressed many people in his community through his harsh tax requirements. Zacchaeus likely also felt contempt for the "common people," who were both his victims and his livelihood.

5. In His mercy, Jesus converts Zacchaeus. He brings Zacchaeus to faith in His forgiveness and salvation, and His love breaks down the tax collector's stony heart to respond in acts of gratitude and love toward others.

6. Accept participant responses. Answers will focus on Jesus' ministry, above all His death and resurrection, as our one hope for salvation. Jesus seeks us; we do not seek Him and "save" ourselves. He is the Good Shepherd who returns the wandering sheep to the fold.

The Catechism

Invite a participant to read the Eighth Commandment and Luther's explanation. Then allow participants to reflect on and answer the questions.

7. Encourage participant discussion. At times, lives are literally destroyed—suicide, wrong executions—by false testimony and lies. In general, society suffers the consequences of unjust and false witness.

8. Allow participants to reflect on and answer the question. Our Christian witness can quickly be damaged when we gossip, spread rumors, lie, and speak untruthfully. Our Christian witness can be strengthened

and enhanced when we speak honestly, truthfully, and with integrity.

9. Accept participant responses. Some answers may include living in trust, forgiveness, love, mutual respect, etc.

God's Word

Invite a participant to read aloud this portion from Holy Scripture. Use the questions for reflection and discussion on the text.

10. Ananias lied when he reported to the apostles that he sold the property for a certain amount, when he in fact sold the property for a higher amount. As Peter says, Ananias was free to use the money as he wished or to donate the money to the Christian church. As a member of the body of Christ, he was not free, however, to lie to God. Likewise, Sapphira lied to the Holy Spirit by participating in the deception.

11. Accept participant responses. The lie threatened the believers' fellowship by undermining mutual trust, accountability, singleness of heart and purpose, etc.

12. Encourage participant responses. The body of Christ lives in the Gospel; it walks in the truth and serves the Savior whose Word affects every part of our life.

God's People Pray

Use the prayer as a closing devotion. If you wish, include special prayers for needs of participants, your congregation, your community, the nation or world.

A Verse a Day

Encourage participants to read and memorize the Bible verse for each day.

6 THE NINTH AND TENTH COMMANDMENTS

Pray Together

Use the prayer as you begin the session.

Discover

Read aloud the session theme.

Introduction

Read aloud, or invite a participant to read aloud, the brief introduction to the session.

- Answers will vary but may include the freedom from material possessions, from the demands of schedules, from elaborate plans, etc.
- Answers will vary. Encourage participant discussion.

The Catechism

Read the Ninth Commandment and Luther's explanation from the Small Catechism. Read aloud, or invite a volunteer to read aloud, the paragraphs and questions on the meaning of the commandment.

Invite participants to share their responses.

1. Accept participant responses. At root, covetousness is dissatisfaction with what we already have.

2. Encourage participant responses. Our houses and farms, in fact, mirror our personalities, interests, goals, etc.

3. Allow participants to reflect on the various ways they can help others to "keep" their property.

God's Word

Invite a participant to read aloud this portion from Holy Scripture. Use the questions for reflection and discussion on the text.

4. Ahab's and Jezebel's sins include, among others, greed, sinful desire (covetousness), false testimony, murder, and stealing.

5. Naboth's death affected his family deeply. They lost their property and may have been reduced to poverty. The larger community also suffered, because no one was exempt from the king's sinful desires.

6. Accept participant responses.

The Catechism

Invite a participant to read the Tenth Commandment and Luther's explanation. Then allow participants to reflect on and answer the questions.

7. Coveting is, in many respects, idolatry: we put other people and objects above God and the gifts He has given us.

8. Accept participant responses. Our family and career give us a sense of identity, purpose, worth, continuity, etc.

9. Encourage participants to share how God uses His people to encourage others to be faithful in their individual callings.

God's Word

Invite a participant to read aloud this portion from Holy Scripture. Use the questions for reflection and discussion on the text.

10. The man was confident of his goodness; he felt a sense of satisfaction about his standing before God and his eternal destiny. The man was also devoted to his wealth; he was unwilling to recognize God's claim on his life above all other commitments.

11. The kingdom of God is the highest priority in the believer's life. Jesus' call to follow Him affects every part of our existence.

12. Accept participant responses. Allow time to share the comfort we have in knowing God's salvation in Christ.

God's People Pray

Use the prayer as a closing devotion. If you wish, include special prayers for needs of participants, your congregation, your community, the nation or world.

A Verse a Day

Encourage participants to read and memorize the Bible verse for each day.